Contents

Introduction

Netball is a game of throwing and catching, played by teams of seven players each. The object is to score goals by throwing the ball through a ring suspended on a goal post, defended by the opposition. The team with the most goals wins. Each player is restricted to certain parts of the playing area and the ball must be passed in order to move it towards the goal.

The seven players depend on one another to move the ball and netball strategy involves a great deal of co-operation between all members of the team - it is not a game where one star player can make up for the limitations of others.

◁ Because the basic skills of throwing and catching are quite simple to learn, netball is a game in which new or young players can master the basic principles quickly and so enjoy playing at an early stage. For very young players, the court area can be reduced and goal posts lowered to make the game more fun.

NETBALL

Wayland

SPORTS SKILLS

Cricket

Gymnastics

Hockey

Judo

Netball

Rugby Union

Soccer

Tennis

Note Traditionally Netball has been a game played only by girls and women. This is starting to change however, as the Netball Association is promoting it as a game that is also suitable for both sexes. Currently, senior games are not played in mixed teams, though in young-player matches, mixed teams sometimes play, with equal numbers of boys and girls on each side.

Photographs by Action Plus, All England Netball Association, Niels Carruthers, Allsport
Illustrations by James Robins and Drawing Attention
Consultant Betty Galsworthy, National Technical Officer for the All England Netball Association

This edition published in 1995 by
Wayland (Publishers) Ltd

First published in 1993 by
Wayland (Publishers) Ltd
61 Western Road, Hove
East Sussex BN3 1JD, England

© Copyright 1993 Wayland (Publishers) Limited

British Library Cataloguing in Publication Data
Lloyd, Gill
  Netball. - (Sports Skills Series)
  I. Title II. Jefferis, David
  III. Robins, James IV. Series
  796.32

HARDBACK ISBN 0-7502-0979-8

PAPERBACK ISBN 0-7502-1699-9

DTP by The Design Shop
Printed and bound in Italy by G. Canale & C.S.p.A., Turin

▷ To compete at top level, you need to be very skilful and fit. You also need to understand the tactics of the game - where to throw a pass, when to shoot at goal.

Netball is a fast and sociable game that is ideal for keeping fit. It is a very popular game for girls and women in schools, colleges and universities throughout the world, particularly in many of the old Commonwealth countries.

The ultimate aim for top players is to be in a team competing in the World Championships that are held every four years. The Championships were once dominated by England, Australia and New Zealand, but strong teams from Trinidad and Tobago, and Jamaica have challenged them in recent years.

Getting started

One of the advantages of netball is that no expensive equipment or clothing is needed. Players wear easy-fit cotton sports shirts with short skirts or shorts. Shoes should fit well as you will be starting and stopping, accelerating and changing direction throughout the game - feet need firm support for this. Training shoes with flat non-slip soles are ideal. Socks should be made of wool or cotton to give your feet some protection against blisters. For outdoor games in cooler climates, a track suit will keep your body warm while you are warming up and stop you getting a chill after a game, while you cool down again.

▽ The goal consists of a post 3.05m (10 ft) high, with a 38cm (15 in) steel ring at the top, from which hangs an open net. The ball is similar to a size five soccer ball. It can be made of leather, rubber or synthetic material.

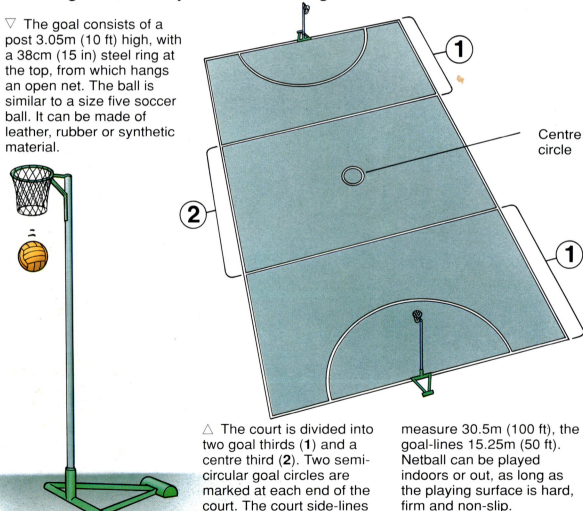

Centre circle

△ The court is divided into two goal thirds (**1**) and a centre third (**2**). Two semi-circular goal circles are marked at each end of the court. The court side-lines measure 30.5m (100 ft), the goal-lines 15.25m (50 ft). Netball can be played indoors or out, as long as the playing surface is hard, firm and non-slip.

Playing areas

Players are restricted to certain areas. Only two attacking players, the goal shooter and goal attack (who score the goals) are allowed in the goal circles, along with their opponents, the goalkeeper and goal defence.

At the start of play, players must be in the thirds of the court shown. One of the centres makes a pass from the centre circle that must be touched or caught by a player in the centre third.

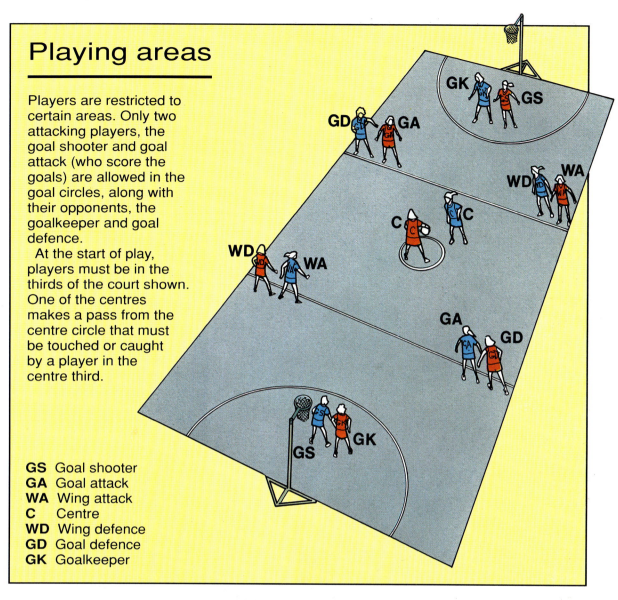

GS Goal shooter
GA Goal attack
WA Wing attack
C Centre
WD Wing defence
GD Goal defence
GK Goalkeeper

▷ For easy identification, players wear bibs marked with their positions.

Rules and umpires

The game is controlled by two umpires who stay outside the playing area, each looking after one half of the court. A full game consists of an hour of play, divided into four quarters of 15 minutes each.

There are strict rules about how you can play the ball. It cannot be passed over a complete third of the court without first being touched by at least one player. The ball must be passed properly - it must not be fist-punched, or handed directly to a team-mate. The ball cannot be rolled along the ground, kicked or passed from a sitting, kneeling or lying position. However, you are allowed to pass by bouncing the ball or to bounce the ball once yourself, before completing your catch.

◁ A toss-up is used to put the ball back into play if offences by both sides have taken place at the same time, or if the umpire cannot decide who last touched the ball when it went out of court. Two opposing players stand facing one another, arms at their sides, looking towards their own goals. They must be 0.9 m (3 ft) apart. The umpire holds the ball between them at below shoulder height, then blows a whistle and flicks the ball up into the air at the same time. Players try to catch the ball or flick it away.

▷ You cannot keep possession of the ball for more than three seconds. Top players have developed excellent timing and balance, making a catch and throw look like one effortless movement.

When you receive the ball you may bat it to another player or tip the ball once or more before catching it. However, once you have control, you only have three seconds in which to pass the ball or shoot at goal. If you fall while catching the ball, you have to stand up again before playing it and you still have only three seconds to do all that.

The footwork rule is another very important part of the game. You have to stop when you receive the ball and you are then allowed to move just one foot, either in the direction of the pass or to pivot and throw the ball (see pages 12-13).

If any of these rules are broken, a free pass is awarded to the opposing team, from where the infringement occurred. If the ball goes outside the court area, play is restarted by a throw-in. This is taken by a member of the team that did not touch the ball last on court.

Ball control

Playing netball is very enjoyable once you can handle and control the ball with confidence. But it is not a skill that comes automatically. Top players seem to have the ball almost glued to their fingertips.

The first step towards developing this ability is to become really familiar with the ball, its shape, weight, size and texture. Pass it from hand to hand, gradually widening the distance between your hands, then taking a few steps to each side as you catch the ball.

◁ Good ball control is the skill of getting a ball under control even when it looks out of reach. It is not just your hands that you use but the balance of your whole body.

Bounce the ball on the ground at various heights and strengths and get used to the feel of it and the work done by your arms, wrists and fingers. Use both hands together, then one hand and the other alternatively. Concentrate on the ball, moving your feet to stay with it. Keep practising until you can keep up these simple exercises for a long time.

Round-the-body exercise

Hold the ball in one hand with your fingers spread wide apart and move it around your body, first to the left and then to the right. Start (**1**) at waist level, moving around your body with the ball, until you are bending your knees and circling your ankles (**2**). Then move the ball up your body until you are circling your neck. Practise until you can twist your hand, wrist and arm around your body quite confidently without dropping the ball.

Ball-spinning exercise

Hold the ball above your head with your fingers pointed backwards. Use both hands to spin the ball (**1**) and keep catching the ball with relaxed wrists and fingers (**2**). Keep your eyes on the ball and move your feet so that you stay underneath it. When you can do this, try the exercise again, with one hand only.

Footwork and balance

When you play netball you have to run fast, change direction quickly, spring for the ball and stop, all in a relatively small space. The key to these activities is good footwork. If you run with small steps with your weight on the balls of your feet and your knees bent you will be much better prepared to make any of the necessary movements.

The footwork rule does not allow you to run with the ball once you have caught it. The ball is seldom caught with both feet firmly on the ground, so when you jump for a ball you need to learn to land and get your balance quickly. When you catch the ball, you may either land on both feet or just one. For beginners, a solid one-two landing is the first one to master.

One-two landing

1 Catch the ball in the air and land on one foot.
2 Ground your second foot in front, to get your balance and control, and to stop any further forward movement.
3 You can move the second, or stepping foot, several times in any direction, pivoting on your landing foot. However, if you lift the landing foot you have to pass or shoot before it is grounded again.

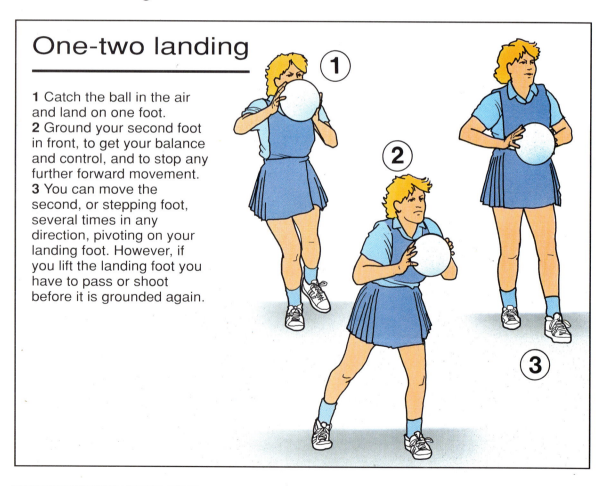

▷ The ability to spring in to the air is very useful because the ball is airborne so much of the time. The higher a player can spring the wider the range of passes he or she will be able to catch or intercept.

When you land on both feet at the same time, you have a choice of which foot you can move. The first foot to be moved then becomes the stepping foot and the same rule as before applies. This may be useful when you are trying to get into position to shoot a goal. However, one-two landings are those most commonly used during the course of a netball game.

If you prefer to throw right-handed, train yourself to land on your right foot, bending your knee to prevent it jarring, and grounding your left foot. Keep your weight on the right foot and step with the left in the direction in which you want to throw the ball. The push of the right arm and the step with the left foot will help you make a balanced and accurate throw.

Catching

Catching is an essential part of netball because the game depends on rapid and effective passing to keep possession of the ball. Dropping the ball and fumbling with it will upset the timing of moves made by your team-mates. Wherever possible, catch with two hands as they are much safer than one.

Good catching involves watching the ball carefully from the moment a player prepares to throw it. As the ball travels through the air try to judge its speed, direction and height.

◁ This player has made a safe and sure two-handed catch at full stretch, with fingers spread firmly around the ball. Notice how, for a high catch, the fingers point upwards. The player's arms have already started to bend and give as they receive the ball. If arms and fingers are too stiff, the impact of the ball may hurt.

Reach for the ball with your arms and body, jumping if necessary. Keep your hands far enough apart to receive the ball with fingers spread, palms facing one another. Catch the ball between your fingers, thumbs and the heel of the thumbs, not in the palms of your hands. Having your thumbs behind the ball prevents it slipping through. As you catch it, bring it back towards your body ready to throw.

△ For this low bounce catch, fingers are pointed downwards as the ball is taken. It is important to learn to catch low bounce passes as they are a useful way of getting past a good defender.

Throwing

Once you have the ball, you must throw it accurately within three seconds. There are a number of different passes you can make, depending on how your opponents are positioned and how the ball is caught. A good throw will be one that avoids any interception and that the catcher finds easy to take. The throw should be aimed ahead of a running receiver so that she or he can run and catch it with outstretched arms. Part of the skill of good throwing is being able to judge the speed and direction in which the receiver is moving.

◁ The halt between the catch and the throw gives you time to get into a balanced position for your throw and to select not only the player who is free, but the one in the best position to take the pass.

All passes have three main parts. The preparation stage, after your catch, where your weight is evenly distributed on your feet and the ball is moved into a throwing position. The release stage, when the ball is aimed and thrown in the chosen direction, using feet, body, arms and fingers and finally, the follow-through in the direction of the pass.

Shoulder pass

This is a strong one-handed pass thrown over a distance.
1 Stand in a balanced position with the ball held to the chest, your feet about shoulder-width apart, weight on your back foot.
2 Turn sideways and take the ball behind your body, at head height, fingers spread well behind the ball.
3 As you throw the ball, transfer your weight from the back to the front foot, turning your hips and shoulders. Use a good strong extension of your arm and a flick from your wrist and fingers. Let your arm and body follow through towards the target.

Chest pass

This is usually a quick, two-handed short pass made to a nearby player. Start in a balanced position (as in **1** above).
2 With your weight on one foot and the ball in both hands, draw back both arms to the chest, with fingers pointing to your head and thumbs almost touching at the back of the ball.
3 Step forward with your other foot, extending your arms strongly, wrists and fingers adding extra force.

Throwing 2

◁ The overhead pass is a two-handed throw. Once you have caught the ball, lift it high, with your elbows bent, fingers either side of the ball, thumbs at the rear. Send the ball forward by straightening your elbows, swinging them forward from the shoulder with a good flick of the wrist and fingers. If you jump as you release the ball you can get more height from your throw - this is called a jump pass.

When you catch the ball over your head, often after a jump, you can use the overhead pass to lob the ball high in an arc over an intercepting player. This can be a good quick throw for a goal keeper or defender to make under the goal-post when they see a member of their team free. It can also be used to pass the ball down the court. However you need good judgement to make this an accurate pass.

Underarm pass

This low pass is useful if you need to throw only a short distance, particularly as the ball can be directed underneath an opponent's outstretched arms.
1 Take the ball from the holding position, down and back, to a position below the hips.
2 Support the ball with the hand underneath and transfer your weight from your back to your front foot.
3 Swing your arm forward with a thrust and release the ball from a low position in front of your body. Your follow-through should be smooth and long.

Bounce pass

This pass also keeps the ball low and is a useful move to make if the thrower has an opponent right in front. It should reach the catcher so that it can be taken at hip height.
1 Catch the ball and take it to your chest.
2 Hold the ball as if for a chest pass, with your hands at both sides of it.
3 Thrust your arms down and forward, aiming the bounce to be beside the feet of the defender, where she or he has farthest to bend to reach the ball.

Shooting goals

No matter how good a team is, if the goal shooter and goal attack cannot get the ball through the ring, all efforts are wasted. All players should practise goal shooting as soon as they start playing netball. Start close to the post, moving further away as you improve. Make your shots curve high rather than flat, as this gives a cleaner entry into the goal ring.

When the basics are mastered, you can go to more advanced techniques - stepping forward, backward or to the side, finding better shooting positions, and introducing a jump into your shots.

◁ You never know which players will end up being best at mastering goal shooting. In the pressure and excitement of a game, a good goal scorer is able to keep calm, maintaining balance and judgement.

Basic shot

1 Take up a well-balanced stance with your weight on the back foot. Your back leg should be slightly bent. Hold the ball high on your shooting hand with your palm turned upwards, fingers spread towards you. The other hand should be at the side of the ball to help with balance.

2 Aim for a point above and in front of the ring, so that the ball drops in a curve.

3 Bend your elbows and lower the ball to head height. Then bend your knees and push upwards with your arm, giving the ball a good flick as it leaves your fingers.

▷ Defenders will try to intercept your shot or make it difficult for you to aim. The defending player must be at least 91cm (3 ft) from the shooter. This distance is measured from the landing foot of the player in possession of the ball. It is therefore useful to learn a shooting action with the landing foot being the one nearest the goal post.

If the defender gets too close, the shooter is awarded a penalty shot or pass, from where the defender infringed. The defender must stand to the side and take no part in the game until the shooter has released the ball.

Attacking moves

When your team is attacking, the aim is to pass the ball towards goal as effectively as possible. Players need to make themselves available to receive passes and this is known as 'getting free'.

A sudden sprint to the side is one of the simplest and best methods of getting free. If your opponent is standing at your side, sprint away on the unmarked side, moving forward to a position where you can stretch to catch the ball. If you make some sort of movement first, swaying with your body or taking a step to one side, you may be able to confuse or unbalance your opponent. You can then sprint off in the opposite direction, a movement known as dodging.

◁ Here, the wing attack has managed to sprint free from her defender and find some space to take a quick pass. The wing defence has been left floundering by the move.

Turning behind a defender

1 You may find that, despite all your best efforts to keep clear, your opponent still remains with you. If so, this advanced sports skill may let you gain a little bit of time.
2 Try turning about, behind your opponent, and sprinting away on your marked side.
3 When you move behind defenders like this, you will often manage to unsight them for a moment, just enough for you to get free.

Protecting space

1 You can often control an opponent's movement by using your body as a barrier, so stopping him or her moving into the area where you want to catch the ball. Stand with your back to your opponent.
2 Then move away with a quick lunge to catch a pass in the protected space.

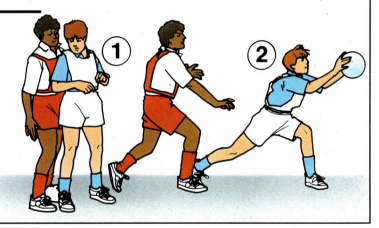

Stopping suddenly, changing direction, running backwards to receive a high pass, dodging and running on are all ways of getting free from your defender. In all these moves, the key is to keep the opposition guessing by trying to avoid signalling your real intentions for as long as possible. When you do move you need to give a cue to the thrower to help her understand what you are doing. When you start a sprint or lunge, signal the move by thrusting out an arm in the direction in which you intend to move.

Defending moves

The purpose of defensive play is to regain possession of the ball, in order to attack and score. When the ball is lost, every member of the team must try to get it back by forcing the other side to make mistakes, by limiting the space in which they can make moves, and by intercepting passes.

One of the main methods of defending is marking. A one-to-one marking system is most commonly used, in which each player is responsible for defending against one other player. This means staying close to, but not touching him or her, so that other opposition players are not sure if they can pass the ball safely. If a pass is attempted you can try to intercept it.

◁ Here, tight marking looks as if it will lead to an interception by the wing defence. Once the ball leaves the thrower's hands, stop paying attention to marking your opponent and go all out to intercept.

△ To mark an opponent, stand slightly in front, your right shoulder level with, and covering, his or her left shoulder. Keep your head turned sideways so that you can see both the ball and your opponent at all times.

◁ In this picture, the wing attack is covering her opponent's ball at the correct distance. By making a barrier with her arms and trying to cover all possible paths of the ball she is making things difficult for the thrower.

If your opponent gains the ball, you can move into a defending position in front. Keep your body moving, your arms covering as much space as possible. Try to assess the sort of pass that is about to be made and its direction, then leap into the path of the ball as soon as it leaves your opponent's hands.

Your feet must be at least 0.9 m (3 ft) from your opponent's first landing foot after he or she catches the ball. If you bump, touch or get too close to your opponent, the umpire will award a penalty pass against you. If this happens in the shooting circle, a penalty shot can be taken.

Teamwork

The individual skills of netball are important, but above all it is a team game. The abilities of the players need to be organized as a unit.

For moves down the court to be successful, players need to know how to get free of their markers and to find space at the right time. The team can plan and practise simple systems of attack which include the order in which each player enters the attack, the direction that players move towards catching points and the next moves after the ball has been passed.

Training like this allows players to use their space efficiently and avoids players crowding together.

△ When your team makes a centre pass, the aim is to keep possession and to pass the ball forward. Occasionally though, a pass to a player behind you can be helpful if others are in difficult positions.

Court linkage

A simple system of court banding gives each player first responsibility for receiving the ball in a certain area of the court. From this system some basic patterns of play, or court linkage, can be developed and practised.

1 Straight pattern.
2 Zig zag.
3 Diagonal or 'Z'.

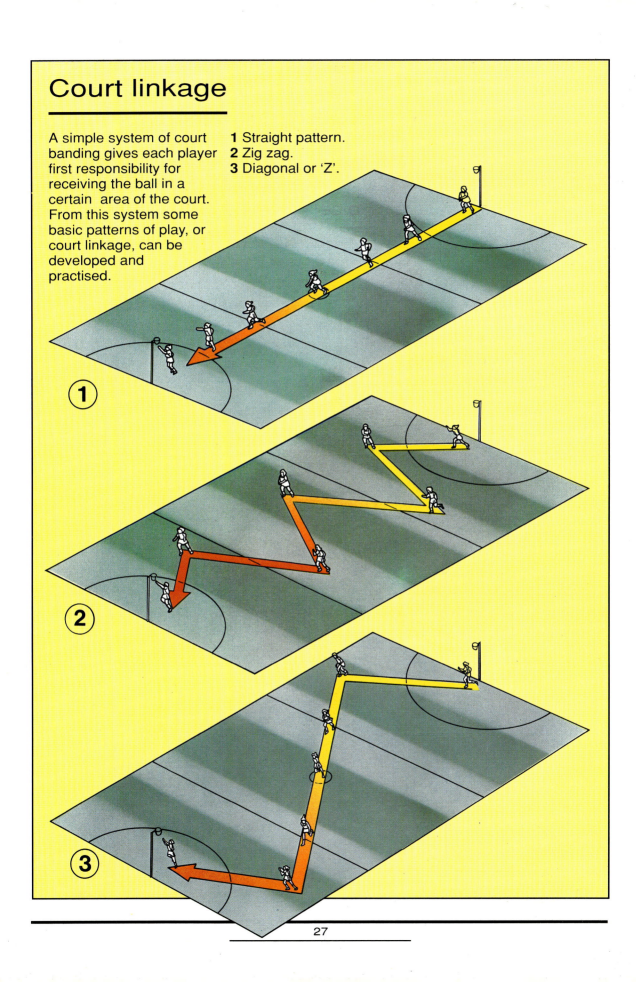

Netball matches

Netball matches take a surprising amount of energy. To play well for a whole game, you have to be fit, so fitness training is an important part of match preparation. Many skills, including throwing and catching, can be practised during training sessions to improve your technique as well as strength and suppleness.

Before a match, you need to prepare yourself physically and mentally for action from the moment the whistle is blown. Warm-up exercises are important to get your body ready for the efforts to come. Jogging, running, jumping and some simple stretching exercises should be a part of pre-match routine. Follow this with some ball practice, such as passing and goal shooting, to get the feel of the ball and to get your eye in.

◁ During matches, players must be able to keep up high levels of concentration, if they want to take, and keep, the lead. Other factors to consider include weather conditions and the presence of an audience.

▷ Knowing the role and responsibilities of a position and being able to blend with the other members of the team is the sign of a good player. Play all the positions before you decide which one in which to specialize.

Glossary

Attacking team
The team that is currently in possession of the ball.

Back-line
The goal lines at either end of the court.

Centre circle
The small circle in the centre of the court from which play is started, or restarted after a goal has been scored.

Centre court
The middle third of the court.

Centre pass
The pass that is taken by the centre to start play, or to restart after a goal has been scored.

Cues
Signals between players that communicate where and when a pass is to be taken.

Dead ball situations
Times during a game when play has been stopped and is restarted with a throw-in, a centre pass, a free pass or penalty pass.

Defending team
The team that does not have possession of the ball. When this team gains possession, it in turn becomes the attacking team.

Dodging
Moving to get away from an opponent.

Dummy run
A deceptive move made by a player who seems to be about to receive a pass, but, in fact, does not.

Feint
A dummy pass in one direction which acts as a decoy to a real pass.

Footwork rule
The rule about the movement of a player's feet when in possession of the ball.

Free pass
A pass awarded to the non-offending team for an infringement of a rule (apart from obstruction or contact). Any player allowed in the area where the pass is to be taken can take it.

Goal circle
The semi-circle that marks the shooting area.

Goal third
The two areas at each end of the court, which with the centre third, make up the playing area.

Holding position
The position of a player in possession of the ball when getting his or her balance and deciding where to pass the ball.

Lines

All lines are part of the court. A ball is out of court when it touches the ground or a person in contact with the ground outside the court.

Marking

One-to-one shadowing of opponents to prevent them receiving passes.

Offside

A player with or without the ball is offside if in any playing area other than that specified for the position.

Penalty pass

A pass awarded to the non-offending side for an infringement of the contact or obstruction rules. The offending player must stand by the side of the player taking the pass and cannot move until the ball is thrown.

Penalty shot

If a penalty pass is awarded to a shooter within the shooting circle, he or she may make a pass or have a shot at goal.

Throw-in

The means of returning the ball back into play when it has gone out of court.

Toss-up

The method used to put the ball back in play when both sides have infringed rules or the umpire is unsure which side to penalize. The ball is thrown up into the air between the two players involved.

Netball organizations

All Australian Netball Association
PO Box 114
Harris Park
NSW 2150

All England Netball Association
Netball House
9 Paynes Park
Hitchin
Herts SG5 1EH

Canadian Amateur Netball Association
21142 Exeter Road
Ajax
Ontario L1S 2J9

New Zealand Netball Association
PO Box 99710
Newmarket
Auckland 10001

Books to read

Know the Game, Netball, Rena Stratford (A & C Black, 1990)
Take up Netball, Joyce Wheeler (Springfield Books , 1990)
For teachers and coaches:
The Netball Coaching Manual, H. Crouch (A & C Black, 1984)
Netball, The Skills of the game, Betty Galsworthy (The Crowood Press, 1990)

Index